D1075125

The Traveling Out and Other Poems

Lucile Adler

THE
TRAVELING
OUT
and Other Poems

THE MACMILLAN COMPANY, NEW YORK
COLLIER-MACMILLAN LIMITED, LONDON

FIRST PRINTING

The Macmillan Company, New York
Collier-Macmillan Canada Ltd., Toronto, Ontario
Printed in the United States of America

Some of the poems in this book first appeared in the
following publications: *Inscape* and *The Desert Review*.
The poem "The Traveling Out" appeared originally in
The New Yorker and the poems "Anita with White
Lilac," "Whisper for K" (called "Whisper for a
Daughter" here), and "Desert Almanach" first appeared
in *Poetry*. Grateful acknowledgment is made to the
editors of these magazines.

for Nat

CONTENTS

PART I

The Stone Bird and the Real

There are two birds on the wall

One has eyes of stone and feathers of stone
And snow melts on its beak.

One has a jet glance and feathers that are feathers
Flounced over the snow.

The children are asked about birds.
"We love them," they promise—the children
Who throw stones, the children who stroke feathers.

One child says the stone bird is more beautiful,
Carved soft and drowsing. Another says,
"I love the live one, puffed out and sleepy in the snow."

Or: "They are both like all birds
But the stone bird is more like all birds."
Or: "Only one can fly but you know
The stone one could if it opened its wings."

The birds are silent on the wall.

"Let's climb up and see," one child says.
"Let's get them," another cries.
One bird peers through the jet slit
Of its eye and stirs. One waits.

Snow falls over the dangerous children climbing,
The woolly children who know nothing of art or life.

Country School

First, children, you may smell the fires
In the fields outside where kernels of corn shine
And the gnarled apples are drying.
That will be our morning prayer.

Now, to what will you pledge allegiance?
To this poor village where the lean cattle
Graze under a sky the color of husks?
To this schoolroom full of cracks for autumn
                              to enter?
(We can never be too open.)
To mountains that are roots?
To harvests of clouds? To cities?
To futures beyond the mountains? Manuel?
You pledge allegiance to Rosa and Toni?
Very well. That will do.

Here is the test for today:
            What is a harbinger?
            What is flight?
            Of what types of flight
            Is man capable?
            Decline the verb "to be."
            What is consciousness?
            (We will expand upon this later.)
            What is the meaning of apples
            Brocading an unsound tree?
            Read from the script of birds.
Rosa, when the bony horses are brought
To the corral and the wind sharpens over the mountains,

What is coming? Cold nights on a mat near
            the rafters of your house?
Simplify. Winter is coming.

Over the rocks the clouds fly;
As over the fact flies the meaning.
Remember this when you fondle seed for the hard fields
Or taste cider from an apple a wasp bit, or
When you run, holding hands or knives
By the knife-strong streams of snow.
Anna, be quiet. Contemplation
Is not only for sixth-graders.

The door has blown open; cold and the corn shocks
Border our narrow desks. Go home through them slowly,
Attend the fires in the fields, concentrate,
School is out. Tonight study the products of Georgia
And your multiplication tables through ten.
Tomorrow again, Discipline.

Peace

The bruja by the gold ash tree
Waits with patience and insanity
For magic to make gold the road
And statue of the senator
Whose stony glare
Put out her mind.

Once lion-colored, her eyes
Are scraped bare and blind now
By the wind that is rising;
Soon pedestals, arms and wreaths
Will fly, and though she forfeit
Even her patience in the storm,
She too will lie among bronze
Brows and shattered leaves
Silently
Unless a miracle from shards
Of wind carves out a shaky bench
Where, broken and blind,
She can wait again
Under the gold ash tree
For magic total as insanity.

Bruja: a witch

6

Charity

Charity walks the worn stones
Of our wonder with eyes the color of water
And her giving brown hands bare.
In a decent dress she wanders,
The rural simple daughter
Whom no one knows, with a flower
Like compassion on the plain bun of her hair.
Beyond the factories of our praise she goes,
Rough hands full of unseen pears
And tough graces for those who hire
Her days; nor does she refuse or spare
Her lyric heart or the shocking pure
And effortless pouring of her ways
As she goes here and there,
The ordinary daughter, fair as water on the stones.

Crusader

Red-cheeked, he rode out
From the home orchard,
On his armor the dark sheen
Of asters; a grubby map of Islam
Tucked under the gleaming mail
His sister polished with moss.

If there was fear
His casque clattered down.

You could tell nothing
But that he was riding out
Bravely, the family banner
Red-black as currants,
His mace ready
To persuade the infidel
Who waited beyond the home farm.

He would be unswerving.

If he saw a girl
At a Circassian inn
Passing baskets of white cherries
Out to pale amputees returning
From treacherous palisades,
She became his most fair
For a time; and he would dally
There among sides of beef
And leafy love, to loot a little,
Then go bravely on,
Unswerving.

Who knows what wonders
He brought back? Silk
The color of asters
To wear under armor. Gunpowder.
Kohl for her eyes.
Who knows when be begot
The red-cheeked son
To roam the apple orchard
On the home farm,
Or how, in the abrasive voice
Of the returned traveler
He warned against
Barmaids at oaken inns,
Too much silk or spiced beef,
Too great a concern over infidels,
And that traitorous notion
That grew up somewhere
About a grail?

Certainties

What she suspects the others seem to know:
How motives solid as the flesh of birds
Shift in a shifty wind and dip
To the ground they all must find.
Everything changes as they stand
Watching the birds, pondering their own
Wings and capacity for flight:

What they know, below their feathered words,
Is how words stand for things that dip
And swing above crevasses in the mind;
They suspect, therefore, there is no ground—
As she begins to grow wings in the bone
To own a vantage others disavow,
And shift suspicion into certain flight
That dips between a snowy sky and snow.

Long Ago

Long ago, little one, a white horse
Grazed on a willow plain
As you rode by asking about death.

Under a milky sky braided with light
The horse leaned over the green furze
That lightened the long red earth;

On that day when hawks trailed
Ribbons of cloud over the sky,
No one could lie to you.

"You will be ribboned with clouds,
You will be water and willow
For a shining horse alone

On a long red plain; you will be wind
Like silk in the mane of the white horse."
For who could lie to you, riding

So sleepily by the willows
Where water gleamed in white pools
On the red soil, holding a wide sky.

Do you remember, long ago,
As the horse flashed by,
How uncompromising we were about death?

Then we braided your pale hair
And let you sleep the rest of the way.

Discovery

The brassbound swarthy ships
Set out, savage, from the sand,
Sailing

Sun-varnished,
On resined winds of the will
To blue kraals of an imagined sea.
Gulls spurt from the mainmast
As the dream-caulked ships
Plow furrows of sand? Of sea?
In this desert.

Sailors with talismans
Of bone whittle delirium
Over holds packed with scurvy,
Stinking hides, casks of tallow and honey
Far from ports in black polar seas.

The sailors sailing
Do not change, ride the teak prows
Baked with endeavor, sweat for the new stars;
Da Gamas, sun-scaled fools in the canvas
Seeking, every child of them, the untamable
Strait to be crossed
As their brassbound ships
Sail past crabbed outposts of the mind:

Always departing from sweltering dunes
To chart the metallic sands
With their bleak debris of old fittings,

They stay on the hot decks
Among ropes tarred with greed;
Sailing, burning on the burning desert,
Bound to their bounteous dream
That goes unslaked forever
As they burn, their natures
Black and burning as what they probe for
Sailing . . .

Duenna to Her Charge

You will be guarded, then given,
Or if not guarded, free,
Or if not given, taken,
But it will all be the same
As seasons of Heaven
You dreamed either free
Or death's true token;
So fire weds stone or flies life's flame.

You will be free, then captive.
Or if not free, then frozen,
Or if not captive, flying
Like flame
Into your melting time; alive
By a hearth where vision
Burns up whole heavens, and Being
Sinks past freedom, free
To kneel; old ring, old name
Plighted forever all the same.

The Guest

The world is crunching
Across snowy stones to the door,
A lantern in its hand, eyes red
With sleeplessness and dawn.

It is pounding at the icy latch
While we lie curled beneath
Our comfort with red wreaths
That helps us resist morning,

Icy water to break and boil,
The chore of greeting day
And the world daily. What urgent
Fists the world has, iron cold outside.

But there are no brown biscuits here
Or blue-checked cloths; no honey.
All the brides to endeavor
Keep their welcomes private.

All the good husbands are
Gone over the rutted fields
Away; we would have slept on
Under the patchwork of dreams they left,

Waiting for the house to warm.
But now this sense of haste—
A guest! Before there are fires
Or we know how to behave with guests!

This is a crucial dawn.
We must knead bread,
Weave our plain names
In napkins that cannot be stolen

Ever, rub our hands with ice
From the cracked china bowl
Till they learn tenderness,
And, as we braid our hair

Beside the stove, memorize
Dreams and childish greetings;
(For this bear of a thing outside
Panting with haste, brings word.)

We must invent the past quickly,
Fling it down for snow-caked
Feet to drip on, then scour
The ashy hearth, fast;

Snatch up the red chair and
Shake out our acts, while
The world waits, sour
With hunger and stern sentences.

Listen, do you hear the pounding,
The harassed guest outside?
Now, now the door swings wide
And in the crack between the open

And our ungainly pride
That has never yet been ready
For the great event, that is alone
In the house this morning,

Appears the worn-out crazy guest
For whom we must provide
A wide embrace, a silence
And a waking place . . .

Portrait with Lemon Leaves

Paint us at home in umber rooms,
Our hands folded over the snowy cloth
Or stroking a child's chrysanthemum head
Near loaves of bread and lemon leaves:

Let our faces be drawn with love,
Hollowed by kisses as mottled stone
Is hallowed by feet passing in
To see something true:

Let our hair, caught by scraps
Of jay blue ribbon, flaunt brightness
When we lean under lamplight true
As homes lit by those who risk love:

If you must lie, let our bones bit
By toil glow tenderly over a shaggy child
Stealing smooth fruit from a bowl;
Let your brush light us, render

The sagging flesh creamy and bronze;
And let us emerge alive, limned with light
As love is; each of us a masterpiece

Glistening from your hands, but authentic,
True as we all are true.

Brother

Honor has every name
Under the sun; my dishonor
Has been your pride, my proud banner
The rag you tied on your beaten head.

To be beaten was to be wise
Or truly bad; and there was no fame
For the runner who brought us word.

Brother, though we did not share
The same wound nor bear the same prize,
Let us join this one time
To surprise and win the rare
Torn rag together, and proclaim

Together our tattered word;
Tie Peace on our ruined heads,
And go crowned with a glorious shame
Down to the death of our time
And honor of our name.

Desert Almanach

How well-connected God is in the land!
His great rock-ribbed relations stand
Avuncular and lava-browed; storm ties
Striping their weathered breasts; rocky
Streams bounding with their brown blood.
Nobility frowns on their right hand.

Eagles crest their vast armoires where bones
Of mutinous small birds are pressed;
Under giant claw-feet, wings like lancets
And manes of common beasts fret the sand.

Stony aunts with amber crosses and insects
On their breasts are claques calling
Him Nephew; they dream how dignity
Once frolicked in coronets of green leaves
Over the bright indentured sands;

Erect now, the color of port, they stand
Quaffing snow from baronial mantels and
Exhorting their scion's presence in the land.
While He, distracted from a flower in His mind,
Frowns and moodily flings down lightnings
And His orb of sun, unimpressed by clamant ties
Or genealogies of stone.

The Traveling Out

I wonder, since we are both traveling out,
If we may go together? Thank you.

You may be sure you will be alone
And private as though I were no one;
God knows, I do not wish to increase your burden.
Naturally, these airports, these blinding cities
And foundry lights confuse you, make you
More solitary than the sight of one lost lamp
Across a bare land promising life there,
Someone over that field alone and perhaps
Waiting for you. That used to be the way.

Feel perfectly free to choose how
You will be alone, since we are going together.
Of course, I never move, I merely hold you
In my mind like a prayer. You are my way
Of praying, and I have chosen you out of hordes
Of travelers to speak to silently, on my own.
I will be with you, with your baffled anger
Among fuming cities, with your grief
At having lost dark fields and lamplight.
It is my way of moving, of praying:—

Oh, not to give you someone like me,
That's all over, impossible, I go nowhere;
And besides nothing is given, absolutely nothing
And no one, only white sermons among
The white of a billion bulbs. No,
Sitting here behind my shutters at twilight
I am stretching over the blazing lanes,

The dazed crowds jostled and razed
By light, only to join your mind and guide you
Gently; leading you, not, alas, to my own lamp across
The fields of the world, nor to a cosy last
Prayer of lamplight blessing the fields of the air
But out into hordes of stars that move away
As we move, and for which your traveling
Prepares you to go out a little more boldly,
All alone as I am alone.

Before the Old Arrive

How hard the years before the old arrive,
And cold the seas along the budding coast;
We must ride out far before we dare to leave
The waves that wrecked what we once longed for most.

For all the years before the old arrive
Are salt upon our lips, and cold, and lost,
Unless we find the face that grows alive
In total flower tolling on the crest
Among cold seas, far from the leaf-crowned coast.

PART II

The Lonely Neighbor

I know you though you go alone
To dine on rinds of love and sorrow
From a round plate like a stone.

I know your face, your flat disdain
At being you instead of star
Alone with hunger on the shore;

I do not mean to stroll your pain
Nor patronize the bare mind
Shining, waiting for a loaf of light;

I am the guest who sits to share
The napkin draped about the stone
That hides your hunger from his own,

A neighbor placed on the white shore
To taste this sorrow and this light
And uninvited, ask for more.

Celebration

We have our choice today
Among the plantations of light
And luminous woods
Where blackbirds sparkle.

We may go into any landscape
For all light is fertile
And awaits our coming:

Though we are peons we may choose to bear light,
To celebrate gravely, to hold our heads high
Under our shady hats with their bright streamers.

A Treaty of Liberation

Where to negotiate?
Not here, the pines on guard
Are black, their loyalty not assured.

We must talk unheard
By so much as a mountain lion
Or suave bird:

Perhaps in an old church
Leaking young roses?
I understand your reluctance;

Some monsignors suppress
Their springs and favor stones;
Too high a price for silence.

No, we can't communicate
From the carved dark close
Of a saint's soul,

Nor base concessions
On a mountain lion's growl.
But there is a desert

Deserted by Zouaves and oil
Where hard mercenary winds
(Which alone can be trusted)

Will bind us paw to paw
Until we drive soft bargains
And make boundless

The boundaries of mind
Through blue ententes of space;
Then radical roses will spring

To speak wild treaties,
And our alliance will rise
Wide among black pines

And birds like flags
From stone, rising,
And men rising, revived
And sovereign.

In Memory of Certain Sapphire Flowers

Let the weak be merciful.

Let them scavenge from the rubble
Of Wisdom a scrap of wisdom to wave
As they ragtag to the barricades,

Where in shattered layers of the past
The fossil flowers grow. There
Let them pluck the absolute color

Of tenderness, last shown in the lives
Of old sages, whose cries of warning
Leaked through history to carve

A memory of wise men lost, and
Certain sapphire flowers saved in stone.
Let the weak raise on their banners

Those invincible flowers, and salute
The old brave men as they charge,
But mildly, blue fields folding over steel—

And charge again in ranks of tenderness:
Lest rotted stem and flame they yield,
And the hard past be acted out again

And the wrong barricades be won:
Let the weak be merciful.
Pray: Let the weak grow strong.

The Dream Stampede

I

At night worlds sink by water holes
And bonfires into silence: bandanas
Are lowered from faces that had to face dust:

After the wind, privacies— Those exposed
Now to darkness turn about in the dark.
Boulders and boulevards hold their breath

As the fiery night subsides on the flanks
Of women, charred wagons, wild outriders
And destinations stalled in dreams.

II

For some the sky rides like leather
Over a sweat-lathered running
Away or over a well-oiled gun;
Not even the stars bridle their anger

That rides out beyond plains and cities
Choked with heroic settlers, sleepers,
Cowards dun as the dust but dark now.

For some, stars spur tomorrow's
Homestead; a white snort of water,
Jewel crude windows in mud palaces,
Sweet gourds of greed: But now:

III

Beasts rouse and hurtle, broken loose
From Time, over blankets askew in each dark.
Questions charge—horned, crazy-eyed herds.

Heroes, wheels, hooves and skies thud
Unlassoed past shaggy historic words:
Uproar cascades over buffalo grass
Matted with night and silence:

IV

In the slow dust on the dark plain
Or town with the wind down, answers
Range wide as space a star goes through
To stake a water hole this night.

A Wedding near Pilar

Among these lava rocks, a wedding.
The bride wears peach flowers
And a hawk circles the running water.

No one knows what is best:
Is it right to carry lighted candles
Before dark across the water?

Or right to break off peach flowers
For a crown, however humble? The hawk
Shadows the rocks with foreboding.

Is it the right season?
Will the bride remain faithful?
The hawk depends on abundant waters

Near the black-clad guests;
The bride will depend—on what?
Does she know what will nourish her,

What is best? Here is a wedding, a spray
Of peach, a jet of water upon rock,
Even a ceremony of wings;

As they light the candles they wait
For the sure-footed groom to step over,
But no one is sure of him,

Or if the wedding should go on
Beside the running water,
Or if it is all for the best.

In the Parish of Cristo Rey

All the dark women common as twine
Rise on the night road bearing candles;
Wrapped in black shawls they wind
Past bonfires and the dying fruit trees
Whose branches are black baskets among stars.

As the dark women walk the winding road
Shielding their candles with thin hands
And bending their hidden faces, the night wind
Begins to stir. Slowly they move now,
Hiding in a bent frieze their old hunger

For birth, for daughters to star the rough bark
Of the fruit trees shawled in night.
The women pause, cupping their secret light;
As the night wind fills its basket of branches,
Their candles bloom on the night road
Like constellations waiting to be born.

Something of My Own

"Very well," the plain man said, "I will go on.
But the day has been drained of something;
A flavor is gone, this light lacks color.
But I will go on without complaint.

Still, if you could hand me a trifle to carry—
One of those green branches a bird just left,
A stone with a mica eye, or glasses for insight—
No, not a sword or a cross, nothing weighty . . .

The wife these days has all the armor, the bifocals
And crumbs; it is she who lights the stubs of candles
And holds the terrier on her lap at twilight.
I want something of my own to carry, you know what I
                                    mean?

Not a key—the wife has had bolts made and uses them
When my grandfather's nickel-plated watch says evening.
Well, I will go on. Would a small bowl do, a bowl
To hold what comes along? But that's just it,

What's left to come to me? The wife, now, is safe;
She'll brew bark tea against my weakness and stay
Behind to lock the root cellar over darkness.
You know what I mean? She could go with her hands

Empty all the way and not mind; but me, I keep
Wondering what the light lacks, and wanting
Something, even an idea to carry, an idea
I could take out of my pocket and hold

When the sky looks incapable of day, lying
There with the brightness let out of its veins
Till nothing matters. Yes, if you could spare
A simple idea, but beautiful, that might be best,

Easier than a bough or a bowl (the bowl
Might seem like begging). I don't complain.
But if you could do me this favor, I swear
I'd go on better somehow, . . ." the plain man said,

And full of all he lacked, vivid with grief,
                          set out.

After Van Gogh

Who can go undaunted
Between the giant sunflower sun
And phlox-white oily whorls
Of heat that blind? Between
Roiled blue grains
Of mountains
And grinding flowers of light?

Who can go on,
Frail as a black cosmos seed
Or hot pollen flake
Of yellow sand exploding

Through turmoil
Of white, of yellow fire
Coiling mountain
And man-form
Into one blind storm
Of cornflower and bone dust:

Who can go undaunted
Towards the far well
And the cold cup
Beaded with reason,
And not be lost?

A Dangerous Stretch

This is a dangerous stretch of road,
Children, where the drunkard sleeps
In the sun, but wakes suddenly

To reach for a white stone or one of you.
Tease gently, children. That yellow sky,
Like the eye of a Monsignor, never sleeps.

I know why the leathery vino is propped
High among cosmos and torn signs there
To tempt you, so sin tenderly, and beware

His brown drunken sleep by souls
Drying like hides on the sunny wall.
He may, crazy, or suddenly penitent,

Reach out, as we all do, I confess,
Parched for your lives to slake
Our own under the tawny sky;

How we wait, propped in the sun
By this dangerous stretch of road, for you
To pass ducking a white stone,

Or running cool as rain from our hands
That reach brown prayers for you,
Children, to tease our waking to sobriety.

The World Came Round

Who promised we would be
What we were meant to be?
The world came round

Our asphalt barred by sun,
And nothing was too late,
And nothing was too soon.

And when a house burned down
We hid our fear inside
And raced about at noon;

And when our brother died
We swung on the black gate
And hid our fear inside,

And it was all a game
With lemon drops for stars,
And we were told Sun's name

And he was ours. Who ended play
And stood beside the gate
Demanding we show joy?

Then everything was hard.
The promise came too soon,
The sun, too late, was tired,

The world burned gayly
Down, our brother died,
And we were barred from play.

At noon when daisies fried
Beyond the iron gate
Time woke and pretense died;

We came to work—to be
What we must humbly be
With beehive industry;

Outside the children play
And when we leave the gate
We cry—"Risk joy";

And sun kneels down to wait
And nothing is too soon
And nothing is too late.

Letter to a Friend with a Bomb Shelter

Dearest Emma,
You cannot imagine how delighted I am
To learn that you at least will survive—
That your good William can provide
True shelter, and that I may have a friend
Left in the world. No woman alive, I am sure,
Is more charmingly fit to observe
What lies beyond shelters when the mountains
That kneel yet on the horizon
Have stumbled to their feet
To collide at the last— As for me,
I am consoled; I feel pride in that pride
Of William's that agrees you are worthy.

(I myself must count on the muscles
Of mountains to hold up my arthritic days
And advise when the horizon I adore wants me.)

In my will I bequeath you smoky crystals
To match your eyes in the dark,
A Ming bowl to sip wry water from,
My black seal stole to keep your ankles warm,
And such seeds as I have saved
From the gold rind of my life.

Who knows what melons
Will grow from those old desires,
To offer sustenance in your new home?

As I near the end of my page, dear Emma,
I must beg you with all your dauntless charm

To beg your honorable William (for my sake)
To disarm:
Lest he mar the gardens you will go to,
And insult the dust of my mountains.

Though I am fussy and old, I wish you well,
Happy to assume that past the flame
Of the altar where I kneel
You will arrive, and live a bit,
And have light left to utter in my name
WHAT A SEVERE MATTER JOY IS,
That must survive our fear, lest
The last world be least and lie bereft.

Whisper for a Daughter

Birdling, be honest.
Say only so much, if more light
Cannot be imagined.

Promise only that which will be;
As, the wind rising,
Trees rising, white waves.

Use a willow whistle
Or be silent if truth interferes
With a salt-bright word.

Sometimes pluck feathers
From the talk of others
To weave into your silence.

Build, little bird,
From your frosty chores
A white perch of candor.

One day, the heart that nests
In your mouth will fly
Out; it will have straight wings,

And it will honor all the silences
Rising to meet it.

PART III

A Cool Place To Go

A lady
With a silk parasol
Appears on the noon sands
Seeking a wise silver stream,
A cool place to go.

Above her stars coil through sun,
Yellow clouds rattle intent
And a black wind forks
Landmarks and her parasol
Away: There is no stream.

Diamond-backed noon
Envenomed with terror
Waits to strike,
To slay her on the sand:

But the lady,
Clad now in yellow fire
As though it were gladness,
Flares forth inspired, knowing
Danger too is a place to go.

As in Tibet

What is happening? What is happening?
In the hill towns the snow is falling
And in Tibet the bells are capped by snow.
Here and there wild ponies run over stones.

A million women kindle fires and lay cloths
For men they love or hate
In clapboard houses or mud houses at twilight.

The mist in the valley is rising.
A great man is out looking for great men.
Someone is stabbing his brother.

A little girl lifts a gray cat with a cat's grace
Into a room out of the falling snow.
What is happening?

They are carving rafters, carving decisions.
A woman with braids changes her love
From one man to another.

Hunters in a remote place climb
Through the mist to caves and ringing bells.
Stews are bubbling; a gaunt face prays angrily.

The nations, in anguish, ban death at frontiers
Where ponies plunge thigh-deep in the snow:
And all the children offer bowls of milk to gray cats.

In a hill town a man and a girl walk,
Enduring, as in Tibet, the hungry hours till night
And then engaging night.

Traveler

If you are all alone, a stranger in a soft hat
Will hear your heart speak through the smoke
Of the train by the black iron railings;

It is he who will offer you a green-plush pillow
As you sink down in a room that reeks
Of tea by the long bead curtain of your mistakes,

Or he who will part the tousled clouds for you
Before you buckle your seat belt over topaz
Cities at twilight where there is no one.

If you are alone, he will open his attaché case
To your grief in a tobacco-colored station
And prepare you with welcome for departures.

Even in the velours dusk of your own room,
He will make you a home under his soft hat
While your heart reaches for his hand, icy cold and in-
    timate.

Who Love To Stay

We must practice with ties,
Untying them, and going away
Where a blue bay and a strange woman stand,
And a multitude, and another way
Of drawing the hair high; where a carved hand
In a blue museum room
Beckons across thronging skies
And warns lest art lie too complacent for these eyes.

We must walk outside ourselves,
Who love to stay, to learn if staying
Is as we surmise, and wander
Lest this staying be excuse
To rest and rest beneath enameled skies;

Go with the multitude, and pause
Where hands lie carved to look at rest
And a strange woman smiles on wanderer and guest;

Then know, our minds like statues' hands
Muscled to life again, that we go forward here,
Apart; and carve out praise like art.

Along This Street and That

I was cast out by my grandchildren
And went to walk in the rain; went
With all the brown wet leaves
In the wind, along this street,
Along that street, as leaves do,
As the old,
With brown spots on their hands,
Pass clean through fall storms,
Who walk forth in their minds, and must.

So I went, and there was no one
Behind windows to take me in:
(They must not, nor must they rake
The leaves when wet, or try
To make of me brown flames
Before I die.) Walk I must
Among leaves myriad as I,
On that street or on this,
Till days like matches strike my wandering mind
And I flake into fire, pungent
As fall and querulous with joy.

Anita with White Lilacs

Anita, before you go home
Under the parchment sky livid
With white and brown stains of thunder,
Put down your lilacs, sit with me
On this creamy-lichened stone awhile.
Now. Nothing is pure white,
Not even those clouds swollen
With whiteness we use to lure you upwards.

The light dust of the road binds your toes
And rises onto the lilacs with their brown stems.
Nothing is pure white, Anita, not linen,
Nor Irish lace, not lilac nor altitude.
Wait here awhile.

Needles of sun embroider noon,
And sweat smocks your gauzy dress
As I admire your dry brown hands
And agate eyes appraising
The clouds that warn you home. Wait a bit:

Passion is always noon, a degree of whiteness
Scrawled through the dark bronze thunder.
You are silent as a brown moth
Tossed in the sun, lost in flecks of light—

If you will stay, Anita, we will place
The wiry stems by your feet in cool water.
Then I will lie to you; cool drop by drop
I will lie, assuaging your thirst

With the damp smell of tales I will guarantee,
And scrolls drawn from the gleaming dust
Of summer mountains steaming with snow.

Anita, rest awhile.
Dig your shy toes in the amber stream bed
Where I will force threads of water
And that coolness I promised.

Then I at least will revive:

While you start home holding white lilacs
In your mothlike hands, trickles
Of water and sun staining you as you go
Slow through your own storm of wonder
At the hot and toppling heart of noon.

The Kite

A dark stick of a boy
Unwound the kite of his mind
From a stick bound with twine
In his hand; a gold dragon
Flared out on white
As he dreamed that he ran,
A dark stick famished for height,
Till the gold fleck of his kite
Rose to become the white wick of the sun.
Dreamed as the wind bit down
The thin twine in his naked hand
And tricked the bright foil of his mind
That the sun flamed at his beck;
Dreamed on, in the flickering wind,
Stock-still and all alone,
A dark stick on a hill.

Overture

Before the death of song men sang.
Then greatness ran like fire on the lips
And sound kissed sound—mind, mind;

We must not sorrow by the pyre of song;
A custom dies, a passion burns away,
And other music waits to seed the wind,

And bear a child whose silver lips
Will play the whisper of a wingéd sound,
A promise soaring past our ashen end

To alter silence with the mouth of joy—
A kiss of fire mastering the mind
In overture to Man, great once again
                              with song.

Forecast for a War Child

An old defeat,
This gold-skinned child
With basalt sores for eyes,
Subsists on crusts of sky,
Never to be deprived
Of his hunger,
Nor of his cold surmise
That any child
Who yanks a marigold
Holds in his fist
A war:

Nor older,
Though he try to rub
Charred bark
And roast
His bare hunger
For a taste of love
Will he be victor,
Able without devouring
To hold in his hand
A dove.

For F. L. H.

Wise men
Call you a great event
That, slow as a seed
Opening
Blasts the resentful clay
To grave
And purposeful flowering;

An event,
An idea in the dark
Waiting
Brave and colorless
As sun
To announce, as sun does
The shocking plain
Truth of day,
What is true and plain:

Waiting,
You may scorn
Blessings
On your hardy "yes"
That needs only light
To flower;
Scorn history
Trumpeting
After the event,
And honors
Common as our clay
In which you wait,

Sad and triumphant,
For death or welcome,
For death and welcome;

But you are a bright act in the land.

A morning glory opens where you stand.

Counterattack

As the threats mount
We study pebbles—those
Grained like wood,
Or discs of stone
Purple as violets
To throw.

My friend moves his hand
In a kind gesture;
I look away from his kindness
Down to the stream bed.

Here is a bone-white weapon,
A stone as big as a gun I could hold.

My friend faces the wind
And the threats that are mounting.
He, too, is afraid, but his love
Lights the faces of stones
As I lean to choose weapons
Prepared by the careless stream:

Though I would fling
Into the legions of threat
A lurid lilac stone
Or one grained like an oak fist,
My friend, with a rueful gesture, laughs,
And turns my arsenal into flowers.

Near Santa Fe—Two Deaths

I

What Remaldo must do as his pain freezes
And the wild ducks sweep low
With coarse cries over the frozen pond,
Is try to go like a great man.
Bells are ringing for an old priest
Who had his own pain. And bells ring
For a frail lady wrenched from her walls
And flesh in the dead of winter. God
Knows if God attends each dying;
Those lying ready to be torn out
Divine their own grief, as Remaldo
Grieves for Remaldo
With hidden icy tears, knowing only
The dark is Dark, the cold Cold.
But he has been told God waits
Above the pond even for him:
And hearing the wild ducks he knows
The air is not too frozen for his flight;
Remaldo will go like a great man dying.

II

The sick man sat in the dark
Under the cottonwood trees;
He was telling someone
About something beyond
The dark soft huddle and spread
Of the irrigated land; he was
Recalling the desert,

And the tribe dancing.
The person beside him in the dark
Was no one, so he told
How his brothers, the dancers,
Feared the eye that could see
And seize the secret name of the spirit;
And he coughed, and a cow coughed
In the waiting dark, and suddenly
He saw his companion, nameless,
But alive and watching, and suddenly
He clutched at his own name,
The one that meant something,
And fear rose, not fear,
But a shaking, and
He said: "I feel like a man
Who walks on a ridge in the wind."

From the Fire

The child asks the fire: "Where do you go?"
As we sit sighing by the hearth.
"Where do you go?" We hear the wild birds
Screaming by, and pant our praise
For blood, air, wings that assault
Those frozen by fear, those fearful of dying.
Who will become a degree of frost
Burning through pelt and feather?
Who will be a cell in the hinge of a wing?
Or an inkling of fire lighting a great mind?
Unbearable to define our own going:
We sip wine as the child by the fire asks:
"Where do you go?" And the sublime weak fire
Cries to the child and the cold
Where wings are beating—"Out!"

Good Night

To all that is alive, good night.
To all who walk in the cold
Knowing their own features,
And to all who go, silent, past
Lamplight not knowing how to share
What is known of the cold
Or of craving and loving:
To loneliness itself, shuddering alive
Outside at night; to the cold,
The livid or calm cold
Thriving over weak men who dare
Dream love beside a fire
And amber hives and honeyed days—
Dreams sleep alone. Nor does cold
Care. But for all creatures
Bearing night, unloved and lost,
For all alone learning to be alone
Past love, who still endure the cold,
A knowing spreads and grows—
The drop of dawn we crave and share.

We Are All Walking the Same Road

I

We are all living at once and walking the same
road on the same cold afternoon. Blue cities shine
in the distance tender as misted grapes, full of lives
tapered and warm as Malagas. The cities are here, and
their lives, mixed with our own harvests, join the walk
home from our blue fields held in by mountains.

II

It is no one's fault that when we reach home we cannot
prevent the cold nor grasp the flames of the great minds.
We dream of them by the hearth in our house on Abeyta,
knowing we all live at once.

III

A great mind? A whole populace in the skull of one man,
working together to construct an Attica solid as sky and
crisp as snow, impervious to Time. The minor great burn
with other fires which we must sort as we do the wools
dyed by pomegranate from those that drank cochineal.

IV

Our homes shine among dark leaves under the mountains.
Tendrils of damp hair, of lives, bend as hunger is served
before the fire . . . for greatness itself or for its
semblances. Prices are juggled, expeditions planned,
wines judged and diluted with snow; someone laughs, and

an old aunt whines for a bunch of grapes before she dies.
She can see them in the blue fire.

V

In our houses life grows like cities with many towers,
like shaking mountains of flame on the hearth, like
piñons slowly. There is nothing to mourn, so long as
each fire is fed, each house faces outward, and each
sleeper under his dyed rug feels the snow of far places
on his face.

VI

Genius though hidden is shared, a secret brandy warming
the throats and veins of strangers. The genius of a time
is the amplitude of humble men who hold such liquor well,
and from a tangled memory of stars and sextants, blue
grapes and seas, blued steel and gaseous silk sails
make marvelous maps showing Abeyta vaster than Asia.

VII

Deep below the Barrier reef, at the heart of the dark
pomegranate seed or the crystal, man walks, we all walk,
molecules in a space that is no longer blue, but familiar
now as lead or sapphire, while the genes grow on a vine
of life that is known. Even we . . .

VIII

It will be tomorrow soon. Time to go out. The wings
of Mercury are folded inside our sleepy heads. Now the
children laugh, are scolded and stuffed by an old aunt
with sugared bread, prepared . . . There is need for
passionate haste, for those wings to open, for morality,
fresh latitudes . .

We are living all at once, walking on Abeyta road
past blue cities and harvests of understanding. Child,
dear neighbor, love, what is it we are sharing, sheer
as the form of our fire last night and related to the
sun whose common dye lights all our faces? There is
no genius in the face of the genius that makes us walk
here, alone of course, but hand in greater hand.